INSPIRE ME INS

'The Beep

BY

DEBORAH CASSAR-EGAN

Feedback and support appreciated at Inspire Me Inspire You

Deborah@inspiremeinspireyou.co.uk

INSPIRE ME INSPIRE YOU

DEBORAH CASSAR-EGAN

Copyright © 2014 Deborah Cassar-Egan

Dedication

This book is dedicated to my mum and dad. Not only for bringing me into this world, loving and caring for me during their lifetime. But also, for looking after me and caring for me in their afterlife.

Preface

I am writing this story to let those who want to know, we are never alone in this world and far from it! In the Spirit World there are many there to help us through our journey in life. I know this to be true by the experiences that I have had since my parents died.

My Mum

It was January 2003 and I was well into my Trade Training as a Personnel Administrator at RAF Halton when my Flight Commander summoned me to her office. She was a Flight Lieutenant and in charge of my welfare whilst in Trade Training. Normally she was smiling and very chatty. On this occasion there were no smiles only sadness in her eyes. She informed me that my mother was in hospital and I had to go home immediately. She offered to pay for a train fare home but I wanted to drive. I needed time to think. Although at this point I had no idea what was waiting for me around the corner.

My mum had been living a fantastic life in Spain. In 2001 when I had left University I decided that I wanted to go travelling around Europe. My mum decided that she wanted to come with me. You can imagine her surprise when I explained to a 49 year old lady who loved make-up and looking good all about backpacking, Youth Hostels and lots of walking. So she came up with an idea, maybe we could rent an apartment in Spain where she would stay and I could use that as a base for my travelling. So we did, we rented a lovely apartment in Fuengerolia in the Costa Del Sol. We had a fantastic time together, so much so that my mum decided that she wasn't coming back to England. She wanted to say there for a while longer. She had made some lovely friends and was very happy in the Sun. I was sad the day I was leaving Spain but I knew my heart was set on joining the Royal Air Force and I would be able to visit her regularly.

Two weeks before being summoned into my Flight Lieutenants office, my dad had phoned me and told me that my mum was flying home for a visit and staying with him. I told him that I would come home that weekend and pick her up from the airport. I remember picking her up at Liverpool Airport, she had lost a lot of weight and looked extremely tired. She had been getting pains in her stomach and didn't want to see a doctor in Malaga she said she preferred to see her own doctor. We managed to get her an appointment and the doctor gave her some medication. The doctor wasn't sure what was wrong with my mum but thought maybe it was a virus or stomach bug. I felt relieved, it was lovely to have my mum home and I knew that my Christmas leave was near so I would be able to spend some quality time with her.

When I was on Christmas leave I stayed with my mum and dad. My mum gave a brave smile and even helped with Christmas dinner. She looked awful when I look back at the photos but I didn't see it at the time. She had gone back to the doctor and got some more medication but still no answer as to what was wrong with her.

The 3rd of January 2003 was her birthday and all the family got together for a drink at my dad's house. My mum had one Bacardi and coke then went to bed. The next day I returned to RAF Halton to carry on with my Trade Training. That was until I got told that I needed to go home immediately.

A few days after I had gone back to RAF Halton after my Christmas leave. My sister had taken my mum to hospital with excruciating pain in her abdomen and she was admitted into hospital straight away. That was when I got told to go home by my Flight Lieutenant. The doctors carried out lots of tests which took almost a week before the verdict was out. I remember us all around her bed when the two doctors came to let us know the results. My mum had terminal cancer of the liver and had one or two weeks to live. My mum looked around the room at her five children, her sister and my dad. You could cut the air with a knife I didn't know what to say or how to react, I was in total shock. My aunty told us all to go outside and get some fresh air, I couldn't move and I didn't feel in control of my limbs. It was like watching a scene from a movie.

Once outside the hospital, my brother, three sisters and I huddled together and cried until our tears ran dry. I didn't want to accept it and I couldn't believe there was nothing the medical profession could do.

My dad was in denial and refused to believe she was dying. I knew I had to be strong for him as he wasn't in the best of health himself. He had suffered with Bronchitis since birth and he only had a quarter of a lung that worked for him. This meant frequent chest infections and hospital visits or his yearly MOT as he called it. He loved my mum dearly and never really got over her leaving him.

We decided that my mum was never to be left on her own so we paired up and took it in turns being with our mum and giving her whatever support we could. The hours were never long enough if only time could stop and wait for me to catch up but of course I had no control. I paired up with my younger sister whom I had a turbulent relationship with from when my mum left. She was only 11 years old when my parents separated and she had stayed living with me and my dad. I was

16 years old and took the role on of taking care of her whilst my dad worked. I understand now that all she wanted at that time was her mum and not her sister. We both sat with a glass of beer and chatted by our mum's bed laughing and joking about old times and past stories. My mum was highly doped up on morphine but she kept opening her eyes and smiling at us both. She even managed to say, 'I'm happy that I've brought my two babies back together', then she shut her eyes again.

We were told on Friday 10th January 2003 about the cancer and my mum passed away the following Friday which was the 17th January. It was all a bit bizarre how it happened as my brother and two older sisters had already said they would rather not be there when she died. They didn't think they would be able to cope and would find the experience traumatic. We had changed shifts at 6am that morning and I was there along with my younger sister Mel and my mother's sister Gilly. Mel had just finished plucking my mum's eyebrows, since they were a mess and my mum used to pluck them every day always wanting to look her best. She was always putting cream on her hands, nail varnish on her nails and rarely did you see her without make-up on. We put some cream on her face and hands then sprayed some Calvin Klein Eternity perfume on her neck. My aunty said, 'Val, you look lovely now, ready to meet our mum in heaven'. With that my mum opened her eyes (which she had not done for three days) looked at Mel, Gilly and then me and took her last breath. 'Cherish' by Kool and the Gang was playing on the radio…my mum certainly knew how to exit the living world.

My Dad

First let me tell you about my dad. For a large part of his working career he worked at his family run Funeral Directors, 'Egan's Funeral Service'. We had many debates sat in our local pub about life after death. He said on many occasions he had tried talking to dead people but he had never had a response. During his training to be a Funeral Director he said that he and his friends had spent nights at a local cemetery to see if there was any activity or ghosts. He wanted to believe but had found no evidence during his life to convince him otherwise. For some reason I always thought there was. It was a feeling within me and so we made a pact one evening sat in the local pub that when he died he had to come back and tell me that indeed there was life after death. Little did I know at that time it wouldn't be long before his time on earth was to end.

It was one week after my mum's funeral, Dad had a bad chest infection and he had to be admitted to hospital. The doctors and nurses did their usual routine, antibiotics, daily physiotherapy on his chest and within a few days my dad was feeling better. I was sat at the hospital bed with him and we were chatting, just me and him. He said I looked nice, I was dressed up to go out into Manchester for a few drinks with friends. I told him that I was glad he was feeling better I couldn't cope with him leaving me too. He said not to worry he wasn't going anywhere (if he could help it).

2am (6 hours after I had just seen him in the hospital ward) I got a call from my sister Mel saying dad has had a Heart Attack and I had to get to the hospital immediately. When I got there Mel, my sister Jackie and my brother Lee stood around his bed in Intensive Care Unit. I couldn't feel my body, I was looking at the man whom was larger than life in my world now looking fragile and small on a Ventilator Machine. Was this really happening? Could life be so cruel to take both my parents away from me within two weeks?

The next day my older sister Jane arrived from London. I was just staring at the Ventilator Machine, please dad don't leave me. At one point I was on my own and my dad opened his sky blue eyes and looked at me with sorrow in his eyes. I knew he was saying that he was sorry. I held his hand and willed him to fight and not to let go.

We were told the next day that he was doing ok and would be looking at leaving the Intensive

Care Unit in a couple of days. However, the next day he had another major Heart Attack and the doctor wanted to take him off the Ventilor as his major organs had given up. We all huddled around his bed, my three sisters, brother and step-sister Corrine. My dad took his last breath on Saturday 1st February 2003 just 15 days after my mum's death. I felt like my whole world had shattered at that very moment. I went into shock, I walked around like my body wasn't mine, I didn't feel like my body was attached to my mind. The world went into slow motion, nothing mattered. I felt like a robot just going along, planning the funeral, sorting out what suit my dad was to wear in the coffin. Luckily with the help of my brother and sisters we managed to hold it together to say good-bye to our dad.

My Mums First Contact

7th February 2005 is a day that I will never forget it had been two years after my parents' deaths. It is 00.30 in the morning and I am in my room at RAF Waddington Nimrod Block ready to go to sleep. I had just turned on my side ready to sleep and I heard a beeping sound. At first I thought it was the radiator so I got up and checked to see if it was on, (it wasn't). I then stepped out of my room into the corridor to see if the sound was coming from outside my room, (it wasn't). All of a sudden I went cold, my heart started to race fast and I could feel a tingling sensation all over my body. I was scared, I felt my mum in my room but I could not see anything. When I say I felt my mum in the room it is hard to explain. I guess it is like when you are little and you get a kiss goodnight off your mum. You know that she has left your bedroom but you can still smell and feel her with you as you drift off to sleep. I started talking out loud, 'Mum if that is you then I am scared'. The atmosphere in the room went calm as though all tension had been lifted. My heart rate slowed down and I started to feel less tense. I talked out loud for over an hour and I did not get any reply at this point, I just felt her listening to me. I remember saying that I wasn't sure if it was me imagining her being there and I would go and learn more about the spirit world to see if I would be able to talk to her and hear what she was saying to me.

The weekend following that experience I went into Waterstones in Lincoln. I headed for the Mind, Body and Spirit section. I had no idea what I was looking for, I just knew that I needed to find out more. I couldn't believe how many books there were, so many to choose from. I picked a book up called 'Working with Spirit Guides' by Ruth White. As I started to read the back of the book I got this really intense smell of Calvin Klein 'Eternity' perfume. This is what my mum had on when she died. I looked around me and there was no-one near me. I walked around the corner and there was a woman stood looking at books. I thought, maybe she has the perfume on. So I pretended to look at some books right near her and I took a few sniffs....no it's not her. I moved back round to the Mind, Body and Spirit section. I am still holding the book in my hand. I open the book and again get a strong sense of the perfume. 'Ok', I say, 'I guess you want me to get this book'. I bought the book and headed back to my room at RAF Waddington.

You would think that I would have been eager to read the book straight away but I wasn't, I think I was scared of what it was going to bring. Not only that, I was also scared that it was me and my imagination conjuring up the whole experience.

The book sat on my book shelf for a few weeks and I did nothing else until I got a phone call from a friend in Manchester saying her mum had been to see a medium and that my mum had come through and said to tell me I needed to go and see the same medium so she could talk to me. Her mum told her Debs mum, Val came through during a medium reading. So I knew it was a sign, I had to make an appointment to see him. I rang the medium and booked an appointment in for Monday 21st March 2005.

My Dads First Contact

3am on Friday 18th March 2005 I woke up to the sound of some very loud beeping. I got out of bed and turned off all the electrical equipment in my room. The beeping was still there. I got back in bed and the beeping got louder and faster. This time I didn't feel scared but my heart started to race. I felt my dad in my room, 'Dad is that you'? The beeping stopped, 'Dad, if that is you can do one beep for yes and two beeps for no'? I don't know why I thought to say that at that moment but I am glad I did. I got one beep, I then carried on asking questions getting a yes or a no answer (one beep or two). This went on for 3 hours, going quiet at some points in which I would ask if he was still with me. I would get a beep to confirm he was. I remember asking him if mum was with him and he said no. I asked him if she was with him in the Spirit world and he said yes. It is hard to explain how I knew that it was my dad and not my mum in the room that night. I guess it was my dad's presence that I felt and it feels different to the presence of my mum.

I was shattered emotionally and physically. I was participating in a charity event that day for a colleague of mine whose baby had been stillborn. I was getting dressed up as a nurse and collecting money at the main gate to the station to raise money and awareness for Sands Charity (Stillbirth and Neonatal Death Charity).

At the end of that day I was still questioning what had happened and if it was all in my imagination or not. Within the two years of my parents dying there had been so many times that I had wished my parents to be with me. At times I really was struggling to cope with the bereavement of both my parents. My first posting was to RAF Fylingdales in North Yorkshire. Right bang in the middle of nowhere surrounded by hills, rabbits and sheep. There were about 16 of us who lived on camp so the social life wasn't good and there were many times of feeling alone. In those times I prayed for my mum or dad to talk to me.

I remember one time in particular when I was feeling really angry. I was sat on my bedroom floor crying, then my mobile phone rang, I picked it up from the table besides my bed. It was ringing but nothing was displayed in the screen, it didn't say 'unknown' it just shown a blank screen flashing as it rang. I answered my phone, there were beeps on the other end, I thought there was something wrong with my phone. I know it stopped me crying and then I fell asleep on my bed.

There had been incidents during my working day at RAF Fylingdales when I really wished I could pick the phone up to my mum and dad for comfort and advice. On one particular day I had a disagreement with my Manager and felt really angry. We had the radio on in our office and the song, 'Cherish' by Kool and the Gang came on the radio, and it was the song that was on the radio in the hospital room when my mum had died. That reminder of my mum gave me the strength I needed at that very moment. It was like she was telling me to hold on, to find other ways to cope. The next day I went in to see my Sergeant and asked for a compassionate posting on the grounds of RAF Flyingdales being too remote. Even today sat writing this I can't believe that someone decided to post me to such a remote location when both my parents had just died.

I was so happy when I found out I was being moved to RAF Waddington. A huge military base with over 3000 personnel. There were also people there that I knew from my Trade Training at RAF Halton. It had excellent sports facilities and the potential for a better social life. My life started to get back on track, I joined sports teams, put my name down for adventurous training and I got a job working on a Squadron which is what I had always wanted since joining the RAF.

Meet Your Spirit Guide

It was the Sunday 20th March and I was getting prepared to see the Medium in Manchester on the Monday afternoon. I went to my room and got off the shelf the book I had bought from Waterstones 'Working with Spirit Guides' which had been on my book shelf for six weeks. The logic in my head was, if I was going to see the medium and I could experience meeting my Spirit Guide then maybe I could confirm that all this is correct. Maybe the medium will be able to put my mind at ease and I could start to truly believe that my parents were still with me. Maybe just maybe the medium would know that I have spoken to the spirit world without me telling him.

So I open the book and I find an exercise that talks you through the journey of meeting your Spirit Guide. I read through the exercise then I pull my desk chair into the middle of my room. In this exercise you imagine yourself going down a path, through some woods, listening to the stream and taking in all that you see around you. I then went over a bridge and in front of me I could see a meadow. The sun was shining and I felt happy and carefree. I walked further into the meadow and in the distance I could see six very large rocks set out in a circle. I walked up to the circle and went inside. The exercise told me to sit there and wait for my Spirit Guide to come.

I sat on the ground with my feet huddled up to my chest. I heard a voice, it was a male voice. 'Hi Deb, I'm John', he then gently got hold of both my hands and helped me up off the ground. The feeling of love, warmth and joy coming through his hands to me was electrifying. I opened my eyes and he was stood in front of me with the biggest whitest smile I had ever seen. 'Well done in making the journey to see us, take your time to slowly adjust'. He then asked me to look at what he was wearing and to try to describe what I could see to him, his outfit; shoes; hands and the jacket he was wearing. He had on a pair of brown shoes, cream trousers and a smart white shirt that had a light blue pinstripe line down it. He told me I was doing really well and even though I couldn't see everything it didn't matter and in time I would be able to see it all. 'I've got a surprise for you' he said holding my hand and walking me to the other side of the circle.

I looked up and there to my astonishment were my mum and dad. I ran over to them cuddling my mum first and then my dad. My mum looked so happy and proud. 'See Brian, I told you she would do it'. My dad hugged me and held my face in his hands, 'Well done Debs it's really lovely for you to visit us'. I was crying with happiness as I never thought I would see them again. I didn't want to let go of them, I could really feel my mum hugging and kissing me. She looked healthy and vibrant, my dad's wrinkles had gone and he looked about 40 years old.

They told me that I could come to the circle at any time to see them. John who was my Spirit Guide will work with me to develop my Spiritual awareness. For now though I had to go back, it was emotional for me and I needed to develop slowly they said. I didn't want to go back, I wanted to stay with them talking and catching up. My eyes were streaming with tears. I didn't want to say another good-bye to them. John held my hand and reassured me that I would be able to see them again. He told me to journey back through the meadow over the bridge through the woods. I opened my eyes and I was crying. I must have sat on that chair in the middle of my room for at least an hour. Did I just meet my parents? Am I going mad?

I wiped my tears away and prayed that the medium would be able to confirm what had just happened. If it was true, the possibility of being able to talk to my mum and dad again made me so excited and happy.

My First Medium Experience

It was Monday 21st March 2005 and I pulled up outside the medium's house in Bolton. His wife answered the door and asked me to wait in the living room. My stomach was in knots, I had never been to see a medium before. I was directed into a room at the back of the house. I walked in and a man in his 50's with white hair like Kenny Rogers was sat on a chair. He asked me to sit down on the armchair next to him. He said something about green, red and yellow colours around my ankles but I wasn't sure what he meant. It was something to do with how he worked with spirits and the colours represented if I was telling him the truth.

'Right, let's start he said, a lady is here and she has put a white rose on your lap and she is saying that she is your mum'. What happened next freaked me out a little as the medium's facial expressions and body language changed to my mum's at times whilst he was speaking. She said I wasn't to buy the Audi TT that I had been looking at. I wasn't to leave the RAF until I had got my Corporal tapes. She thanked me for the photos, letters and white rose that I put in her coffin. She was really proud of me and to stop thinking that this was all in my head. She talked about our time in Spain together and how happy she was there. She still had the necklace with her that I had bought her for her 50th Birthday present.

Then my dad came through and told the medium that I had his ring in my pocket (which I did). I had taken my dad's ring with me as neither of my parents left a will and I was down as their next of kin and I had no idea who to give the ring to. My dad told me to give the ring to my oldest nephew.

As I looked at the wall opposite me I could see outlines of people. A glowing light, no faces or features just outlines. I told the medium this and he said, 'Yes I know you can see them, you have a gift and you need to take care of yourself and learn how to nurture that gift'.

I left his house feeling refreshed and relieved that it wasn't all in my head. How else would he know that my mum and dad had died and that I had my dad's wedding ring in my jeans pocket? I was really sceptic going into my very first medium experience. I had put the ring in my jeans pocket to test the medium so I was relieved that my dad came through and told me who to give it to. I sat in my car outside his house and wrote down everything that I could remember him saying.

I headed to my sister Jackie's house to tell her all about it. She was slightly freaked out to say the least. She said that her taps in the kitchen kept turning themselves on, especially when she was trying to have a cheeky sleep on the sofa during the day. Apparently, she would close her eyes and both the taps in the kitchen would start running water so she had to get up to turn them off. She wondered if it was mum telling her not to be so lazy and to do some housework. My mum was always tidying the house so I guess that sounded exactly what my mum would be saying to her.

At the time it was really hard talking to my siblings about our parents. We were all dealing with it in our own way. I had seen a bereavement counsellor whilst I was still at RAF Flyingdales who really helped me to accept my parent deaths. I was so thankful to be able to talk to someone about it, that lady really helped me in the biggest upset of my life.

I drove back to Lincoln that Monday evening. I went round to my partners and was talking about what the medium had said. The lights in the room started to flicker. I could feel the presence of my dad listening to what I was saying. I felt really excited and ready to move forward with my life. I knew I needed to discover more, I certainly wanted to find out how to develop myself spiritually.

The Start of Meditation

I had never meditated before or had a clue what I was meant to do and what I could expect to happen. I read up a little on the internet, how to breathe and to start by focusing on a single object so you could quieten your conscious mind of all the chatter. This wasn't easy but what I did find is as soon as I sat down closed my eyes and listened inwardly I could hear my mum. I couldn't see her but I could hear her voice. About four weeks after I had seen the medium I was lay on my bed and I could hear my mum 'Debbie Doo's, Debbie Doo Doo's'. I told her that I was listening and she started talking about my brother and sisters and gave me messages she wanted me to pass onto them. I was to stop worrying about what other people think and to enjoy myself. She said that life was precious and full of lessons to be learned. I needed to go with the flow and cherish all the good times as I never knew what was around the corner. She told me that my Spirit Guide John would help me if I wanted to talk to other spirits. At this point I was still thinking it was all in my head. I hadn't completely accepted that I could talk to my mum or hear her voice.

Another way of communicating with spirit that I learned was to use a candle. I would sit in a quiet room with the candle lit. I would then ask for a sign for 'Yes' and watch what the candle did. For me it flickered very fast side to side. When I asked for a sign for 'No' then the candle stayed nice and calm, just gently swaying from left to right. I can't remember where I got the idea to do this from. I know I used the candle at the start to get my mind focused. I had read on the internet somewhere and it told me to focus on the flame. When I did that I was able to forget all the other thoughts that were running riot in my mind. This didn't always work, sometimes my conscious mind would not silence and I would lose concentration. When I did manage to slow my thoughts down I could then ask questions to get yes and no answers. I used these in times that I needed guidance and the candle really did work for me.

When I found it hard to focus and my thoughts were coming thick and fast. I would imagine my thoughts being an old vinyl record playing on a stereo. I would then lift the needle off the record and put the catch back on. Every time a thought came I would again lift up the needle and place it back onto the catch. I guess it was training my mind to control my conscious thoughts. It was these moments when I was able to speak to the spirit world.

Sometimes I would hear my guide asking me to concentrate or to not allow my mind to drift. I had to stay focused on what I was trying to achieve. Your conscious mind can be like a child wanting sweets when you have said no. It is not easy to quieten your conscious mind and it takes lots of practise.

Most importantly, it was during this early time of meditation in March 2005 that my mum told me I needed to write my experiences down in a journal. That is all she said in the beginning, just to note it all down so I had something to reflect on.

My First Orb Experience

Thursday 2nd June 2005 I was reading in bed and I could hear a frequency noise a bit like the beeping I heard when my mum first visited me. This noise was a lower frequency, the beeping was slower and not as loud. I got the candle out and lit it, 'Mum, Dad, Are you here'? The candle just stayed calm and didn't show any reaction. I blew the candle out and turned my lamp off. The frequency noise was still in the room.

I looked up to the corner of the room and I could see a blue round glow, which had orange and yellow around the edges. It started coming towards me, it was about the size of ten pence piece. As it got closer to me it then went back to the corner of the room and slowly moved towards me again. It did this about 5 times the same cycle. Fading as it got near me then starting again in the corner and moving towards me. I asked my partner to get the camera, I then had a digital photo taken. You could see straight away looking at the screen on the camera that right above my head was an orb.

For those of you reading this who have never heard of an Orb. My description would be a circle of energy. There has been lots of debates about Orbs and some saying they are speckles of dust that is captured in a photo. I am not an expert in the field of photography, but wouldn't it be the most bizarre coincidence that just as I was seeing an orb that a photo was taken and right above my head is an orb? I will leave it up to the reader to make up their own mind about what they think.

What I will say is this was my first encounter of an orb and it wasn't my last. I was then able to use orbs that I could visually see on a daily basis to help me answer questions that I had in my life. I did this by getting a piece of paper and writing down the people I knew in Spirit world, my mum, dad, nana and Aunty Edith. I then at the top of the paper wrote YES and NO putting it all in large capital letters and dividing my page equally into boxes with the names. When I meditated I closed my eyes to get into a relaxed state then when I opened them again an orb would be in the room. Sometimes two, three or four would be in the room at a time. I would then ask them to show me who was in the room and the orb would then go to the piece of paper to give me an answer. For example if my mum was there then the blue orb would go on the paper over her name. This was very exciting at the time because not only could I hear my mum but I could see who else was in the room. I would also ask yes and no questions and an orb would move to the paper over the answer either yes or no.

I didn't read anywhere to do this exercise, I just felt once I could see the orbs then I could use the paper as a tool to communicate. I found this a very useful tool at the beginning of my spiritual development.

River Elk

On Saturday 4th June 2005 I went to a Mind, Body and Spirit Event at Lincolnshire Showground. Whilst walking around looking at the stalls I came across a gentleman who was an artist and drew your Spirit Guide. Being curious I thought I would have it done since he also gave a reading as well. I wondered if he would draw my Spirit Guide John. I didn't see the drawing until it was finished and it was of an Indian called River Elk. The artist told me that he was one of my Spirit Guides who was going to help me on my spiritual development. Around the portrait of River Elk he drew my aura which told him a few things about me. He said the green symbolised that I had a good heart and the yellow meant that I could think too much. He told me that the blue symbolised psychic ability and I needed to develop and learn more about myself through workshops. River Elk was the one to take me to the next level and I needed to learn to listen to him. This was really interesting for me because although I knew I could speak to John my Spirit Guide when I meditated, it also meant that I had someone else to develop me further.

I woke up early the next morning to the sound of beeping. When I opened my eyes I could see a bright white square on the wall in front of me. I asked if River Elk would show me some more. I could then see a male face in the square which scared me a little as I had never seen a face before this point. River Elk must have known I was scared as the frame and face disappeared as quickly as it arrived.

I put the portrait of River Elk in my study which is mostly where I meditated to speak to my mum and dad. On Thursday 23rd June I was in my study meditating and I got a picture of River Elk right between both of my eyes. He asked if I could hear him and I said yes. He then told me to stare at the portrait of him on the wall. The portrait became 3-D and looked as though a bright light was shinning behind River Elk. I felt like River Elk wanted to test me and to see what I had learned so far. I could hear his voice, he asked me what could I smell? I then got a very strong joss stick scent right near my nose, a musty woody smell. He told me if I smelt that in the future then I am to know he is with me. He then asked me to concentrate on the portrait and to tell him what I could see. As I looked, the portrait changed, River Elk changed into an image of different people. The images kept changing and to be honest some of them looked a bit scary, completely from way back in time. River Elk told me not to be scared, none of those people were in the room. He then showed me some symbols in the portrait of a bell and a key. I said thank you to River Elk for the lesson. The joss stick smell went as soon as River Elk had gone.

Frustrated

It had been five months since I had the first contact with my mum and dad. To be honest I was feeling really frustrated. Maybe a little impatient, I had so many questions and the answers weren't coming quick enough for me.

I meditated to ask the questions that I needed answering. I closed my eyes and I was immediately met by my mum and dad. Remember in chapter five I talked about following the path through the woods to the meadow? Well, I was on that path and as soon as I got into the woods my mum and dad were sat on a bench waiting for me. They asked me to sit next to them and I was surprised as normally I needed to go through the forest to the meadow in order to meet them. This was the first time that I didn't have to do that. I started to cry and my mum was cuddling me. She told me that I was frustrated and I had learnt so much in five months. She said there was no need to feel frustrated and that everything was happening just as it was meant to.

Mum said if it was all getting too much them being around she would give me a break. They were staying around to guide me and it was important for me to let them know if it was too much for me.

My mum said I could see things because I had developed myself spiritually. Some people can hear things, some people can see things, we are all different but we can all communicate with the spirit world. They didn't live on earth, they had their own place on a spiritual plane. It would be impossible for her to be with me all the time, they don't have the energy to do that. She said in time I would understand more and my questions will be answered.

My mum told me that part of my frustration was also my work. I am my own talent, people want to be around me and they listen to me. She said that I had a good background academically to set up a business. I am my own worst enemy and I don't believe in myself. I needed to exercise to get myself feeling fit and healthy. She could see me being a 'Life Coach', talking to people about bereavement and helping them through their life's journey. Dad told me to start a course in massaging or life coaching and to save as much money as possible as I would need it later on. My dad had his stern face and told me that I needed to get my backside in gear. My job was easy and I had weekends and evening to study. They gave me 2-3 years to get my business up and running.

Where Have I Met My Spirit Guide Before

Sunday 7th July 2005, I was reading the 'Meet Your Spirit Guide' book by Ruth White and I came to an exercise called, 'Where have I Met My Guide Before?' I was intrigued by this and I thought I would try the exercise to see what happened.

The outcome was very interesting indeed. Part of the exercise told me to go into a beautiful garden, at the end of the garden against the wall would be a mirror. I was to look into the mirror to the time and life of my Spirit Guide.

Next I felt myself walking up some stairs with a brick wall on either side. There was a door at the top, I knocked on the door and a lady opened the door. I ran inside and sat at a table. I could see soup on the stove and smell the lovely scent of bread being baked. A man was sat in the corner of the room watching me smoking a pipe. I knew he was my 'Pa'. I was a boy about 5 years of age.

There was another knock on the door and an older boy about 8 years old came running in and sat next to me. My name was Chanpa and his was Dankrou I knew he was my older brother. I got up from the table and walked into another room which was our bedroom. There were two sheep skin rugs on the floor and a leather knitted blanket with a candle at the side. My brother asked my Pa, 'What is wrong with Chanpa and why is he acting strange'? To which my Pa replied, 'He is getting to know who he is and how to be able to listen to his wise being'. I had some soup and bread then my Ma kicked us both outside to play. I ran down the steps and saw my reflection in the mirror. I was then back in the garden where I walked to a seating area and grounded myself. My Ma had a lovely warm smile but she said nothing to me, just smiled. She wore a robe and I felt her love as soon as I stepped into the room.

When I brought my awareness back to my own room I was a little dazed. Had I just viewed a life that I had lived in the past? Was that my Ma and Pa? Why was I a little boy?

I went on the internet and looked up the names Chanpa and Dankrou. Indeed they were Indian names. It was all very bizarre and confusing. I knew I was booked in to see another medium in Lincoln on Tuesday 12th July. Maybe she would be able to provide me with some answers.

My Second Medium Experience

On Tuesday 12th July 2005 I visited a medium in Lincoln. I have to say she was exceptionally brilliant. I had never met this woman before, I had picked her card up from the Mind Body and Spirit at Lincolnshire Showground.

She had a very calming presence and I instantly warmed to her. She led me upstairs into a room that had two chairs by a window. Looking around the room she had various qualifications on the wall that I was facing. She started by explaining how she worked and asked me if I had any questions. The session then began, she told me in my career I needed to be brave and make a move. I can choose self-employment and setting up my own business. She could see me doing Aromatherapy, Reflexology or Bowen Technique.

As she was talking she started to look uncomfortable, like she was struggling to breathe. She told the spirit to take it away from her and that she got the message. She then said, 'I have a gentleman here, he suffered with his chest, quietly spoken but would show he was angry or annoyed by the tone of his voice, it is your Dad and he is telling me that communication has been passing between you both'. I nearly fell off my chair, she had it spot on. The medium then said her feet felt like they were stuck in mud, 'Debs do you feel like you are stuck at the minute'? Of course the answer was yes. She then said my dad was lifting me up and frog marching me out of the room, telling me to pick my feet up and to get all the relevant information I needed to move on. I started to laugh because that is exactly the sort of thing my dad would have done and said. The medium told me that you don't always get 100 percent assurance in life and I needed to take chances to discover the job that I would really enjoy.

My dad told her that he didn't want to leave when he had, that he wasn't ready. He had left things unsettled and that we needed his support. He was really happy now because he didn't know or understand that he would be able to help his family from his life after death. He no longer had any pains or aches and therefore he could be more effective in helping us.

The medium was then being shown a key to a house. She asked me if I had just bought a house. I had, four weeks previous to the session.

I needed to get a website up and running, look at how to become a therapist or coach. I needed to raise my awareness, if you don't ask for the help then you won't get it, ask and you shall receive. She said if I ask the spiritual world for help then I needed to keep looking for the reply, the response could come in the form of magazines, television, dreams or even someone that I meet. 'Stop thinking everything that is happening is a coincidence, there is no such thing as a coincidence'.

I didn't want to leave, this lady was amazing and so comforting to be around. I left feeling like a weight had been lifted. I had a new sense of purpose in my life.

Mum's Words of Wisdom

A few days after I had seen the Medium in Lincoln I went into my study to speak to my mum and dad. They showed me they were there with two orbs that were blue with a yellow and red circle. I asked them to come and meet me in my circle I needed to talk to them. As soon as I started my journey I could see mum and dad stood waiting for me. I didn't even need to go through the woods. I felt that my awareness was developing, I didn't need to go through the woods, over the bridge and into my circle anymore. As soon as I relaxed I found that my parents were already there waiting to speak to me.

I was happy to see my mum and I wondered why only my dad had come to see me when I visited the medium. I asked my mum why and she said she had jobs that she needed to do and therefore couldn't make it. She wasn't concerned though as she knew my dad was going. I wondered what jobs she needed to do. She certainly didn't need to hoover up or do any cooking. I noted that in my mind to ask her another time.

We found an area to sit down on the grass and my mum began to talk. She told me that I was on the right path. I said I felt a million times better than I did before seeing the medium, I had more of an idea of where I was going. She told me that I was going to be successful in my career. Dad was right in giving me a push forward in the right direction and what they admired about me was once I was on the right path they knew I would plod forward on my own.

My mum told me that in years to come I would look back at my journal and realise that mum and dad were right in their advice. They know my path but they can't tell me, I've got to discover it myself. She said everyone has a lifespan and you never know when your time is up. I've got to accept the good times and ride with the waves, cherish the special moments, look after the people in my life and not to take things for granted like she did. Life is like the sea, the ebb and flow of the waves, the rhythm of life that can crash when obstacles confront us. However, it is those obstacles that teach us the most important life lessons. It is about finding ways around or through the obstacles just like the sea does when it hits a rock.

My mum gave me a huge hug which made me cry. As she rocked me back and forth she told me that they will always be my parents and will always be looking out for me. That I will always be her baby, that premature baby that she thought she was going to lose. A mother never loses the love for her child even in death.

When I opened my eyes I was crying because I missed them both so much. I missed surprising my mum with flowers and gifts, I missed chatting about everything in life with my dad. I loved them both so much although it had been two and half years it still felt like yesterday. Even being able to talk to them upset me because it reminded me that they were no longer on this earth plane. Should I feel grateful that I could see them? Maybe, though at that particular moment it hurt to say goodbye, to open my eyes to my world and to remember that they were not with me.

Like a Photo Negative

It was a Sunday evening and I was watching a film in my bedroom. Just above my TV screen I could see a purple square with two spirits inside it, I can only describe it as looking at a photo negative. There were colours of purple and blue and I could see the outlines of two spirits which weren't my mum and dad, I had never seen these spirits before. Maybe they were just watching me for entertainment I didn't know.

They showed themselves about three times moving away from the TV and onto the wall. I was really trying to make out if I could recognise them but I couldn't. This was the first time I had seen spirit in this way and it was magical. I knew that if my mum and dad shown them in that way then I would definitely be able to recognise them.

The next time I meditated my dad was there to greet me. I told him how spirit has shown me the negative picture and why hadn't he done that. He told me that he hadn't learned how to do it. He said your physical body dies on the earth plane but then there is a lot more learning to take place in order to evolve. In time he will be able to do that and he will show me as soon as he has learned how to.

I asked him about his birthday and what he got up to. He said he visited all of his children then spent the day in his garden. He doesn't celebrate his birthday he said every day is like a birthday where he is.

I opened my eyes and I could see three orbs in my room. I closed them again and asked my dad who was with him. He told me to close my eyes and to walk further down the path. When I looked up I could see my mum, she was holding hands with someone whom I couldn't make out. As I got closer my mum gave me a hug and told me that my Aunty Edith was here to see me.

I had never met my Aunty Edith, I knew that my mum and she were really close. When she had died it gave my mum a real shock, she was pregnant with me at the time and it brought on her pregnancy. I was born premature weighing only 2 pounds. Apparently my dad could hold me in one hand and my body went from his finger tips to the end of his palm. So I was really interested and excited to meet my Aunty Edith for the first time.

For some reason I found it really hard to see her. She told me to take my time and slowly I could see that she was wearing a brown skirt with a brown jumper. Her hair was wavy, she gave me a lovely smile then hugged me. She told me that she had been warning my mum about not looking after herself but she wouldn't listen. She had blown the candles out in my house a couple of times and she was helping my mum and dad learn. She told me it was important for me to know that my mum and dad were learning as much from me as I was from them. She had a lot more energy than they did because she had been dead longer. She had the power to turn lights on and off and to move things. In time my parents will be able to do the same.

I told my Aunty Edith not to go moving things about in my house. Also, not to go turning the lights on as it wastes my electricity. She smiled at me and told me she wouldn't. I gave her a hug and said I hoped to see her again.

William Mason

Friday 12th August 2005, I woke up remembering a dream that I had. It was a really strange dream, a guy called William Mason introduced himself to me. He was in a tailored suit and looked very smart. He was smiling at me and introduced himself as Mr William Mason. In my dream I sat up in my bed and looked around the room that I was in. It was far from the modern room of the twenty first century. I was in a four poster bed and the room was huge. Looking around the room the curtains looked old and heavy. I said hello to him and I didn't at all feel scared. He stood by my bed smiling and just looking at me. Then the door opened and a lady walked into the room. She had no head, now I was scared, she had her head in her arms. She introduced herself as Vicky.

Next thing my mum appeared in the dream, she was shouting at me. What! What's wrong! My mum told me never to speak to Vicky again. That she couldn't always be there to protect me. I didn't speak to Vicky and she didn't say anything to me. Both Vicky and William then left the room and my mum was stood in front of me. I asked who William was and she said he was a writer in the eighteenth century. She said he was a friendly spirit but Vicky wasn't and she had told her not to bother me again. That made me chuckle, my mum is so fiery and protective of her children. I certainly wouldn't have wanted to be on the wrong side of her.

My mum said it was important to close my energy down before going to sleep and I needed to learn how to do it. She said I was a good spirit therefore I shouldn't attract any bad spirits. That did scare me a little, William was really friendly but why did Vicky come and see me? And how did my mum enter the dream to warn me of the danger and give me more advice?

Mum was right, I certainly needed to learn how to close my energy down so I wasn't open to any spirit coming into my energy field when awake or in my dreams.

I had a similar sort of experience in September 2005 whilst I was staying at The Jury's Hotel, Manchester. I woke up in the middle of the night and I could see the face of a man right in front of me between my eyes. I closed my eyes but he was still there. I turned over and pulled the duvet over my head but he wasn't going. I didn't like it because I was in a hotel and not in the safety of my home. I asked him to go away because he was scaring me. Luckily he did and I have found when I ask spirit to leave me alone generally they do.

My Naming Ceremony

Wednesday 5th October 2005, I had not written in my journal for three weeks. It certainly wasn't because nothing had happened. I felt the spirit world with me all the time, during my working day and in the evenings.

I had decided that I was going to meditate and ask if there was any other spirits that wanted to say hello to me. I said I would be happy to speak to anyone as long as they wished me no harm.

I started on my footpath walking towards the forest and felt that there were people walking behind me. I turned around to see my mum and she told me to look behind her, although I couldn't see any faces I could see outlines of people. I could hear River Elk talking to me, he told to me carry on walking through the woods to my circle. When I turned around the again I could see that my dad had joined the crowd of people following me.

I arrived at my circle which is where I first met my Spirit Guide John. River Elk was there waiting for me. Next to him was my mum and she was holding hands with two children. She bent down to the little girl and told her that I was her daughter and to go and say hello. The little girl who was about five hugged my legs, she had blonde hair in pigtails, she said her name was Amy. The boy who looked about four years old he told me his name was James. My dad was now stood next to my mum watching my reaction. I wasn't sure what to say, I was confused, why did they have children?

I didn't have long to think about it as people started appearing through the gaps of the rocks around my circle. They formed a circle around me, River Elk came over to me and told me there was nothing to worry about and it was my Naming Ceremony. I didn't understand, what did that mean? River Elk told me that I was being named as a spiritual helper. Then a guy called Jim came from the circle to talk to me, I noticed that he had black shoes on but I was finding it really hard to see his face. I felt nervous so I immediately opened my eyes and returned to my study. I didn't understand what a naming ceremony was and I wasn't prepared for spirits to gather around me for some ceremony I knew nothing about!

Looking around my study I could see movement and hear a fast frequency sound. I apologized and said thank you to everyone that came to see me. I could hear River Elk talking to me and telling me not to worry. I was developing well and in my own time. He said not to worry about the naming ceremony he apologized and said he should have prepared me for it. Then I heard my mum tell me that she loved me and to go and pour myself a glass of wine (sounded liked a perfect idea to me). I guess they would have to do the naming ceremony another time.

My Guardian Angel

Sunday 16th October 2005, I was in my living room it was 8:45pm. I decided to go and meditate as it had been a while since the experience of my Naming Ceremony. I went into my study, before I started I could see the blue circle with orange, red and yellow inside it. But this time it went quite large and ended in a bright deep red which looked lovely. It was extremely fascinating to watch. Also, the lovely bright red circle was in a large purple square and wherever I looked in the room the circle appeared.

I closed my eyes and started walking on my path to the woods. I felt a woman's hand hold mine, her hand was slender, warm and soft. I felt a feeling of pure love radiate through my body. The only other time I had experienced that before was when I first met my Spirit Guide John back in March.

    I asked who she was and she replied by saying her name was Jane and she was a Guardian Angel. She was dressed in a white long skirt and a white t-shirt. Her hair was brown, straight and very long and shiny. She looked about 30 years old. She told me that lots of people were here to speak to me and to give me advice. Looking into the distance I could see a circle I felt a little nervous. She told me not to be worried, they were bringing me words of love and the people only wanted to help me. I asked her why a circle and did I have to sit in the middle? She said I didn't have to sit in the middle and there was no reason for the circle it just made it easier rather than people queuing. I could choose who I wanted to speak to.

    I sat down with Jane on my left and felt a hand grab mine on the right. I instantly knew it was my mum's hand. I looked at her and she smiled, dad was holding her hand and Amy and James were on the other side of my dad. Jane told me to sit and pick someone out of the circle and they would come and sit opposite me. Weirdly all the people in the circle had their heads down. Jane said don't pick with your eyes pick with your heart.

I closed my eyes and said I would like to speak to a man named Jason. He was then sat opposite me, he said he was 21 years old. I asked him what the message was and he told me to slow down driving on the country roads. He said I go too fast and he had died in a car accident. He got crushed in his car because he was going too fast. I thanked him for his advice.

I then got an older lady who came and sat opposite me. Her name was Patricia who wanted to give me career advice. I kept losing communication and I didn't really understand what she was saying. I asked how she had died and she wouldn't tell me. She said that is not what she was there for. She was talking about setting up a business and I can only describe it like a long distance phone call. I heard bit of the information but it was distorted. Maybe I didn't want to hear what she had to say at that moment in time. I know I was able to give my mum and dad a hug. Then Jane walked me back, she didn't hug me, she just smiled.

On Sunday 30th October 2005 I was again met by Jane. She asked me why I was nervous and I told her I didn't know. She asked if it was because someone that I had known had died recently and if I was worried whether I would see her or not. I said I wasn't sure. She told me that I had no need to worry, I had lots of support and guides around me to look after and protect me.

We walked and talked whilst I relaxed my mind. She then took me to a very large circle of people which was two layers wide meaning there was a lot of people there. Again they all had their heads lowered so I couldn't see their faces. Jane told me that it was up to me who I wanted to speak to. I asked if the person that I knew whom had died recently was there and she said yes.

The lady that I knew who had died of cancer at a very young age was sat in front of me holding my hands. She told me that when she died there was a Spirit Guide who took her to see all her family and friends. When she got to my house she asked the guide why there was so many spirits around my home. The guide told her that I was learning to communicate with the spirit world and they were learning to communicate with me. She said she had lost contact with some of her friends in her life and was saying sorry. She had thought it would be easier to lose contact with people and then departing wouldn't be so hard. She told me to pass a message on, to say that she wanted Abba 'Dancing Queen' at her funeral. She said it was strange being in that new world but she would get used to it. She felt set free, healthy and energetic and she had not felt like that in a very long time.

I opened my eyes and thought (what was that about)? Why do I keep doubting myself and telling myself that this is all in my imagination?

Mum and Dads' Spiritual Home

It was a week later when I meditated again to speak to my mum and dad. I could hear a voice as I arrived on my path, but it wasn't a voice that I had heard before. He told me to start walking on my path, he said I needed to relax and let go of everything that was on my conscious mind. I concentrated on allowing my thoughts to pass by and drift until I had nothing on my mind. I then arrived at a gate, the sort of gate you would see whilst walking in a National Park or a Devonshire village. I went through the gate and in the distance I could see a cottage. The guide was telling me to describe to him everything I could see. I said it was a thatched cottage, with a lovely green door. It had the most beautiful garden I had ever seen.

As I got closer to the front door I could see my mum stood there. She had the biggest smile on her face. I knew that the house belonged to my mum and dad. I walked in and the guide was asking me again to describe everything that I could see. I described the hallway, kitchen and living room. A dog came bouncing up to me, it was Lassie our family dog who died aged 18. It was so lovely to see her and to be able to give her a huge hug, I loved that dog so much and spent most of my childhood within her watchful eye. In the kitchen there were thick oak beams on the ceiling, the worktops and cupboards were a dark oak wood. My dad was stood in the kitchen wearing jeans and a shirt, he gave me a wink and a smile. In the living room there was an open fire with two large red sofas. There was no TV but lots and lots of books. I noticed some books on Anatomy and Physiology and I asked who they were for and my dad said they were his. He had been joining me on the massage course that I had started in the September and was improving his knowledge so he could help me if needed. That made me smile, there were so many books and I couldn't read what they all said. My guide told me that in the future I would be able to take a book off the shelf and be able to read the name of the book and the author.

Dad wanted to show me his garden, I could hear the sound of water trickling as I entered the garden. He had a lovely waterfall surrounded by the most colourful flowers. Dad sat in his recliner chair that I had bought him and told me that he had brought it in his mind to the spirit world.

Mum showed me photos of me in my RAF in my number one uniform and pictures of my graduation. There were photos of their children, grandchildren and family around the living room. When I went upstairs there was a room with Amy on the door and another room with James on it. Mum said that they were both growing up nicely in the spirit world and mum and dad were looking after them until a member of their family came into the spirit world. I asked my mum if other people look after children who are in the spirit world when none of their family are there yet. She said no-one is on their own in the spirit world. When a relative of Amy or James comes into the spirit world then they will be re-united.

My dad told me how lucky I was to be so young and to know about the existence of the spirit world and that they are there to help me. Dad said people just plod along in life and never even know that there is life after death till they get there.

He told me to carry on with my massage course and that it will serve me well. But is not the end goal for me, I will eventually find the job that is perfect for me. I was to keep meditating because there was so much to show me. I gave them both a cuddle and opened my eyes back to my home study.

The next time I visited my mum and dad's spiritual home was on my mum's birthday 3rd

January 2006. I wanted to meditate on that day so I could wish my mum happy birthday and to give her some flowers. At first I tried using the sheet of paper that had yes/no with the spirits names on. Nothing was happening, I felt this was because they didn't want me to use the paper. They wanted me to visit them. I started focusing on relaxing my mind and body and then I was at my mum's front door of her cottage. She opened the door and gave me a big hug and I wished her happy birthday and passed her some lilies. There was a crowd of people in the house so she asked me to go upstairs with her out of the way. She asked me what had I been up to? I said did she not know since she has been with me. My mum told me that she only visited me and couldn't possibly be with me all the time as she had work to do as well. I asked what she had to do in the spirit world, she told me that she had lessons to go to and that she had jobs of helping people.

My dad came up the stairs and my mum told me to go and speak to him. He asked me to go for a walk with him. He said he knew a lovely place to sit with a superb view. We chatted as we walked and he told me never to stop learning as that is why mankind is on the earth, to learn and to pass on new knowledge to the next generation. He said I had to get my head down and work hard as it was the only way to get good results. I had a good business mind and I am excellent at working with people. As soon as I got started on one venture it would lead onto another. He told me that he was proud of me and that I should be proud of myself.

We arrived at a fantastic view of the sea with hills and forestry to the right hand side, he told me to look out and admire the view. Life is full of possibilities and I need to take the plunge and go full steam ahead. When we arrived back at the cottage people were stood on each side of the cottages pathway. They were all shouting hello and waving at me.

I opened my eyes and reflected on my journey, I needed to believe in myself. I was doing the Massage course for a reason. I just didn't know the reason, I knew I had to put all my effort into studying both academically and spiritually.

Too Much

I didn't write in my diary for eight months. It wasn't that nothing had happened because the spirit world didn't stop showing itself to me. I think partly the reason was it had become too much for me. It had been causing restless night's sleep waking up hearing the vibrations in my bedroom and seeing outlines of spirit whilst trying to sleep. I felt that I was encouraging any spirit to follow me and it was making me feel exhausted.

On the 16th August 2006 I asked a local medium to come round to my house to see what she picked up and if she could help me. Her visit was very helpful she told me that there was lots of communication going back and forth with me and the spirit world. They had been working with me on a conscious and subconscious level. She said if I was feeling exhausted by it all then I needed to come to some agreement with the spirit world that suited me. I agreed to allow the spirit world to develop me whilst I slept as long as they recharged my energy levels so I awoke feeling refreshed instead of tired all the time. I would start to meditate again and let the spirit world teach me only when I had opened my chakras. The medium taught me how to shut my chakras down and how to open them up for communication. I was to imagine my body in a suit of armour for protection when I wanted my body to be protected, then imagine taking it off when I was ready to speak to the spirit world. She also showed me how to clear my chakras of any negative energy. She went in every room of the house dowsing the house of any negative energy. I really felt the difference when she left, the house felt much calmer and so did I.

I tried it that night before going to sleep and it certainly worked. I woke up in the middle of the night and although I knew spirit was there it was a lot calmer and I was able to quickly go back asleep.

Even during the day at work, I practised putting on my armour and it felt like I was protecting my energy field. It was also interesting that people around me at work could sometimes be negative and that didn't affect me either. Normally it would drain me and I felt that this armour of protection really stopped negative energy from zapping all my positive energy. I was so thankful for the information and learning from the medium.

2005 and 2006 had been very interesting years in my development. I had followed my guidance and finished my Swedish Massage course. I had also signed up for my Diploma in Aromatherapy and Sports Massage. I was able to hear my mum and dad talking to me now without going into meditation. When I meditated I could see them clearly and what was around them. I had stopped using the candle and paper in order to get answers, I felt that I could hear the answers clearly so there was no need to use them as tools to communicate. I felt relaxed and happy.

The Second Stage of Development

Thursday 19th October 2006, I was meant to be flying off to McGuire Air Force Base today but it has been delayed 24hrs due to bad weather conditions. I believe it had been delayed for a reason. When I got home it was in the forefront of my mind to watch a film that I had been told about. The film was called; 'The Secret' and I found it very inspirational. It really made me think about my life and what I wanted from my journey. I sat down and made a list of quotes that was in the movie and a list of what I wanted. The film was about following the Law of Attraction, what we wish for we will receive. If we put positive intentions out into the universe then they will come true. I decided that I was going to put this into practice, I made a list of what made me happy, what did I have that I was really grateful for? I was to ignore anything negative and to channel all my energy on the positive.

    I then sat down to meditate feeling positive and happy. I was instantly met on my path by a guy named Alex whom I had never met before. He was a lovely smiley happy guy, he congratulated me on reaching my 2nd stage of development. He held my hand and then I was on a stage sat in a chair with Alex sat opposite me. When I looked out into the audience they were clapping me. I asked Alex what was this all about. He told me that I was to write a book one day about my spiritual journey and it would sell millions of copies. He said that I had chosen my spiritual path and I would be a Motivational Therapist doing one to one consultations and lecturing to audiences around the world and writing books. My Sports Therapy, Massage and Aromatherapy are a way of teaching me about the human body and how it is healed physically, mentally and spiritually. My job is going to be to inspire, motivate and teach others how to get on the right path with the help of the spirit world. I will cover some work through mediumship but mostly through one to one consultations. He said I have chosen this path and I was meant to watch the DVD and affirm to myself what I could achieve.

My dad and mum was in the audience my dad stood up and said I need to keep learning and using the spirit world to guide me on my journey. He came up and gave me a quick hug followed by my mum who also gave me a hug. Then both went and sat down in their seats.

Alex asked me what I wanted to achieve. What areas did I need help with? I said I wanted to pay my mortgage off by the time I was 36/37yrs old,

I wanted to have a house by the sea with full length glass windows so that I could view out onto the sea and to have steps at the end of my garden leading down to the beach. I wanted my own business as a motivational speaker. Mostly, I wanted health and happiness for all my family and the people that I loved dearly.

I thanked Alex for speaking to me and everyone in the audience for coming to talk to me. I then opened by eyes, nearly an hour had passed by. I have no idea how time can fly so quickly during meditated when it only felt like ten minutes.

I logged onto my laptop and looked at books on Motivational Speakers. I then purchased a book called, 'FabJob Guide to Become a Motivational Speaker' by Tag Goulet. I couldn't wait for it to arrive, was this the job that I would be doing in the future I wondered?

I Can Fly

Thursday 8th February 2007, I'm in trouble yet again for not writing in my journal. I have been meditating but I have not been writing it all down. I am trying to piece my path together. I bought a couple of books whilst I was in America in October 2006 one of them was, 'Awaken the Giant Within' by Anthony Robbins. What a fabulous book it certainly motivates you to reach your goals in life. I feel like I am being guided down the pathway of a life coach, some sort of therapist. I feel like I need to meditate to get some more clarity on the situation.

    I closed my eyes and started my meditation. I became aware that I was in a therapy room. There was a two seater sofa to the left hand side of me and my mum and dad was sat watching me. Opposite me was a lady called Ann who had a clipboard in her hand. She said it was her job to go through my past and remind me of my skills, talents and experiences that have helped me develop. She talked about past memories in which I had helped others feel at ease. She gave me examples of my confidence and what people have complimented me on in the past. She said everything happens for a reason and all of those experiences have given me the knowledge to help others.

Then, a guy called Ian sat next to Ann and he gave me a plan for the next 5-10years. I am to finish my college courses and to set up a business doing therapies. That will put me in a position in which I am able to help others. I will have my house by the sea and my own business. My main earnings in the future are going to be motivating people to break through whatever obstacles they are facing on their journey. The spirit world is there to help me all the way.

Next thing I was stood on a cliff looking out towards the sea. I stepped off and to my amazement I was flying. It was such an exhilarating experience, all I could think of was how lucky were the birds to be able to view the world and its beauty everyday like this. I was able to manoeuvre myself up and down and change directions it was fantastic. I could hear a voice saying look at me, I am able to fly and they will never let me fall.

I felt so lucky to be in a position of being able to experience these things. I could really help people move forward in their lives. This is what I am destined to do and the spirit world is going to help me achieve my dream. Exciting or what!

Mother's Day

Sunday 18th March 2007 (Mothering Sunday), I thought I better meditate and speak to my mum today otherwise I would be in trouble. I also wanted to speak to her about some experiences that I had the week before whilst skiing in Austria. I woke up at 3am whilst in Austria and felt the pressure of someone sat on the bed besides me. I was asked to put my hand up in a stop position. I could then feel the pressure of a spirit pressing against my hand. I could also see a white hand and arm in front of me. This scared me (probably because I wasn't in my home environment). I asked the spirit to stop because I was scared. He said I had nothing to worry about, he was just showing me something that I had not experienced before. The room then went quiet and I was able to go back to sleep.

I closed my eyes to meditate and I could feel my mum's excitement of me visiting her. Then a wave of sadness came over me and I started to cry. I could her say, 'Come on Debbie Doos, wipe your tears away I am here waiting for you'. I closed my eyes and did my usual routine. I was then stood in my mum and dad's kitchen. She gave me a huge cuddle and told me she loved me. We talked about me learning to ski and how I made her laugh, she said I was like the woman from Bridget Jones diary. When I was learning to ski I could see outlines of spirits in the sky watching me. My mum said I was being too adventurous at times and she was worried that I was going to seriously hurt myself.

She thanked me for the plant that I had bought her for Mother's Day that I had put in my garden. She said it would take pride of place in her spiritual garden and my dad will nurture it for her. My mum asked me how I was getting on with my courses. I said I had completed my Swedish Massage, On-Site Massage, Hot Stones Massage and would complete my Sports Therapy and Aromatherapy in July. Mum said that was good news the universe is moving quickly for me. She advised that I would be promoted at the end of this year or beginning of 2008. She wanted me to get my Corporal tapes before leaving the RAF to set up a business.

My mum loved it that I could visit her on Mother's day and she was going to visit the rest of her children to see how they were getting on. My dad came over and said they were both very proud of me and really glad that they could speak to me. I've lots to look forward to in life and I should feel proud of myself. My dad said to keep on working hard or he will be giving me another kick up the backside (charming).

Leaving the RAF

It was my dad's birthday a couple of days ago so I wanted to meditate and wish him belated birthday wishes. The past two weeks had been a whirl wind of major decisions in my career and I haven't known if I was coming or going. I feel like I am starting a new chapter of my life which both excites me and scares me. I went to see my Flight Lieutenant and told him that I was handing my notice in. That I wanted to set up a business in Holistic Therapies and although I love being in the Military it is not the job that I feel is right for me. I needed to be working with people and helping them in times of difficulty. He said I needed to formally fill the forms in and send them off, I would then be told how much notice I needed to give. I could be anything from 6 months to 2 years depending on manning in my trade.

I had had a session with a medium on 17th July and she really helped and motivated me. What was strange is I found the tape from the first session I had with her and it was 15th July 2005 how bizarre that it was within 2 days 2 years ago that I last seen her. She was spot on with everything she said about how I was feeling. My dad came through giving me some reassurance that everything was going to be ok and I had all the skills and talents to achieve my dream.

I closed my eyes to speak to my dad and next thing I was on a stage. My mum and dad were sat on a sofa next to me. It was basically a life coaching session with an audience. A gentleman who didn't give me his name said one day I was going to be stood in front of an audience talking about my journey. How the spirit world has helped me and how I am now able to help others. I liked the idea but at the same time it also scared me. Me in front of a large audience talking about my journey!

He told me I needed to really start looking after my health, eating the right foods and doing some more exercise. He said it was important to have a healthy mind and body if I was to work with people. I had to make a list of my goals and maybe put together a visual board so I could see exactly what I wanted to achieve. He said use magazine or the internet and really get a good visual board together that I can look at every day. There will be no stopping me once I truly believe.

2008 Messages

March 2008 I got a signal through from Man HQ saying I had been promoted to Corporal and I was going to be posted to RAF Marham in Norfolk. (My mum was right by saying the end of 2007 beginning of 2008 for my promotion). However, a little too late since I had already handed my notice in and got a leaving date of 4th September 2008. Also, there was no way I would have gone to RAF Marham so thankfully I didn't have to. My mum would have been happy though as she wanted me to be promoted before leaving the RAF to Corporal so I guess she sort of got her wish.

2008 was to become an interesting year. When I was in Plymouth I arranged to see a medium that I had never seen before. He was brilliant; he said I needed to take my career seriously now. By August 2008 I would have a clear plan of what I wanted to do. He said I would be working with people's energy that I am very intuitive. He could see me with a Complementary Health Centre doing holistic therapies, workshops and breaking people from their limitations. People are waiting to see me and I need to keep positive.

He said don't underestimate the power of thought, you create what you think.

Another night, I went out on works night out and a few of us ended up at a colleagues home whose wife had recently died of cancer. I was talking to him then I got an overwhelming feeling of sadness and I could hear his wife talking to me. I was passing on everything she was saying to me, repeating her words to him. It was really upsetting as he had never experienced anything like this before. I know that everything I said gave him some comfort to make some decisions that needed to be made and he was thankful for me giving him the message.

Another time in 2008 I was at a wedding and we gathered into the hotel bar at the end of the evening. Most people had gone to bed so there was only about eight of us in total. I was talking to the bride's mum and dad when a younger gentleman came through and he was asking me to pass a message onto them for him. I didn't know what to do, you can't just say excuse me I have message from a dead person! I pondered for a while and then I asked the lady if she believed in life after death. She said very much so. I told her I had a guy here who wanted to tell her something. It turned out to be someone she had known that had died in his twenties. She said I described him perfectly down to exactly the clothing he would wear and his personality.

My Book through Meditation

One of the last meditations in the journal was on 26th August 2008. I lay on my bed at home and asked the spirit world if they could show me my path. I heard my spirit guide saying, 'Debs you have chosen your path, go with your own intuition don't think that we are writing it for you, you are a free spirit and you make your own path'. I closed my eyes and realised that I was in an airport. I had a pair of cream cotton trousers on and a white shirt. I felt really relaxed and happy, with a bounce in my step. I was stood looking at the departures board, Singapore Airlines to Hawaii. I then went and sat down for a coffee. I opened my laptop and looked at the presentation I was doing. I had lots of files with presentations on them. Some of them were Find your True Self, Make life work for you, When the going gets tough, Business Mind.

I pulled a book out of my bag and it was called, 'Inspire Me Inspire You' by Deborah Egan. I read about the author on the back and was amazed to see my picture there. The book was my story of how the spirit world had guided me and inspired me in life and how I was then writing it to inspire others who needed guidance and encouragement. I was going to Hawaii to promote my book. Then a lady called Jenny came over to me. She said she had read my book and would I sign her copy for her. I wrote, 'Dear Jenny, thanks for reading my story, Debs'. She said it had inspired her to go and see her sister in Australia who she had not seen for 20 years.

Next thing I was walking out on to a stage and there was a very large audience. I started talking about my journey. I felt really confident, excited and very happy. When I left I called at a bar which I co-owned with a guy called James. It had the most amazing view of the sea. It was a wicker bar will huge chairs to chill, relax and read. I ordered a Mango Surprise which tasted delightful.

Review

I had been writing in my journal on and off for over three years. I didn't always note down when I had meditated and what had been said. To be honest sometimes I just couldn't be bothered to. I wish I had written it all down since so many interesting things had happened. I was told by my mum to write a journal of the experiences a long time ago because I was going to need it when I was writing a book.

By the end of 2008 I had completed courses in Swedish Massage, Reiki Level One and Two, Sports Massage, On-Site Chair Massage, Aromatherapy Massage, Hot Stones Massage, Baby Massage, Trigger Point Massage, Neuro-Muscular Techniques Advanced Massage, Preparing to Teaching in the Life Long Learning Sector, Assertiveness, Controlling and Managing Stress. I had certainly been a busy bee for 3 years and I felt ready and prepared to set up my holistic business.

You see, life has its ups and downs, peaks and troughs. We are all here to fulfil the journey that we have chosen. It has been 9 years now since I started writing in my journal and I truly believe we have angels, guides and loved ones that have passed away rooting for us to achieve the best we possibly can. My parents, guides and people in the spirit world gave me the motivation and belief to achieve my dream. Through visualization and guidance they have taught me that we are all one. We are all here for a purpose and we need to trust our inner wisdom which will help guide us in the right direction.

There is so much that has happened since that last meditation I wrote in my journal in 2008 to 2014 spiritually for me. But hey! I wouldn't want to spoil the next book.

EPILOGUE

When my parents died my life felt like a jigsaw puzzle that had been smashed apart. Pieces had got lost and I didn't know how or where they were so I could put the puzzle back together. I felt lost, abandoned and very much alone. At times I didn't want to be on this earth and wished I had also died. A part of me felt like it had, I didn't feel whole anymore.

Then my mum and dad contacted me. At first I thought I was imagining it all and it was all wishful thinking. Logically I was thinking that my mind was creating it all to help me through the grieving process. My mum told me to start writing a journal of my experiences. Then I got told one day during meditation that I would write a book about those experiences. I didn't think I would write a book but I did think it would be a good idea to write it all down so I could remember what had happened.

Slowly I began to find the missing jigsaw pieces. The difference was, the pieces had changed shape, sizes and the picture on the puzzle had changed. The picture was now of a complete spiritual me, a whole person glowing in love and happiness.

I've written this book so I can inspire people to be open about life after death. To know that from my experience our loved ones are still here for us. Not only that, we have angels and guides who are around us all the time to help us achieve what our soul is destined to achieve. If we truly listen, practise and open our minds our lives can be that of a complete jigsaw puzzle.

Printed in Great Britain
by Amazon

32696497R00050